ELEMENTARY PIANO
Piano solo with optional accompaniment

JEWISH FESTIVAL SONGS

21 well-known Hebrew melodies

Compiled and arranged by
RENEE and DAVID KARP

Editor: Carole Flatau
Cover Design: Marcela Perez

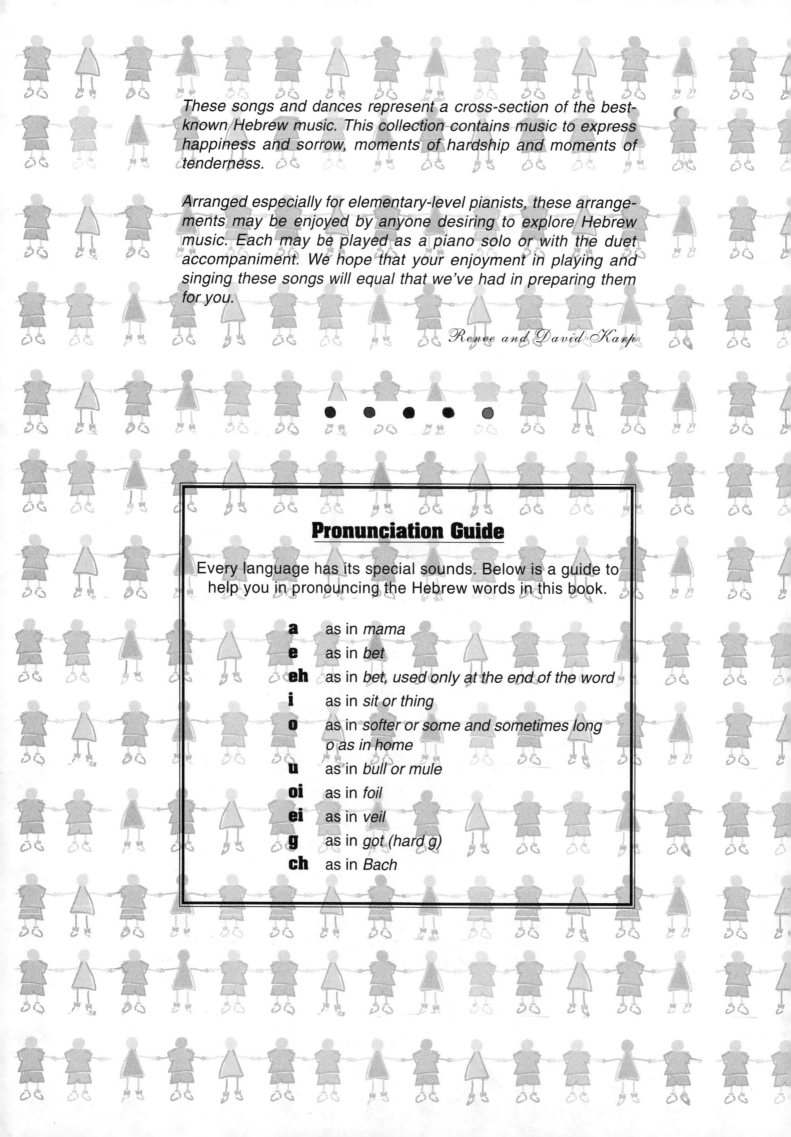

These songs and dances represent a cross-section of the best-known Hebrew music. This collection contains music to express happiness and sorrow, moments of hardship and moments of tenderness.

Arranged especially for elementary-level pianists, these arrangements may be enjoyed by anyone desiring to explore Hebrew music. Each may be played as a piano solo or with the duet accompaniment. We hope that your enjoyment in playing and singing these songs will equal that we've had in preparing them for you.

Renee and David Karp

Pronunciation Guide

Every language has its special sounds. Below is a guide to help you in pronouncing the Hebrew words in this book.

a	as in *mama*
e	as in *bet*
eh	as in *bet, used only at the end of the word*
i	as in *sit or thing*
o	as in *softer or some* and sometimes long *o* as in *home*
u	as in *bull or mule*
oi	as in *foil*
ei	as in *veil*
g	as in *got* (hard g)
ch	as in *Bach*

▲ Contents ▲

For intermediate arrangements, see **Hebrew Holiday and Folk Songs** (EL96112).
For advanced arrangements, see **Chanukah, Folk and Festivals** (EL9545), available at music dealers.

CHANUKAH

Spinning dreidels, lighting the menorah, and eating potato pancakes
and jelly donuts are some of the fun things done during the holiday of Chanukah.

Happily, but not too fast

TRADITIONAL
Arranged by DAVID KARP

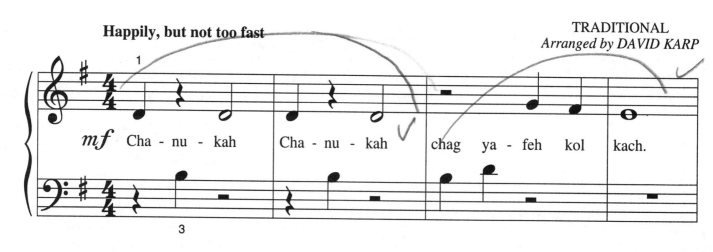

mf Cha - nu - kah   Cha - nu - kah   chag ya - feh kol   kach.

Or   cha   viv   mi - sa   viv,   gil   l' - ye - led   rach.

Accompaniment (*student plays one octave higher*)

9

Cha - nu - kah   Cha - nu - kah   s' - vi von sov,   sov,

13

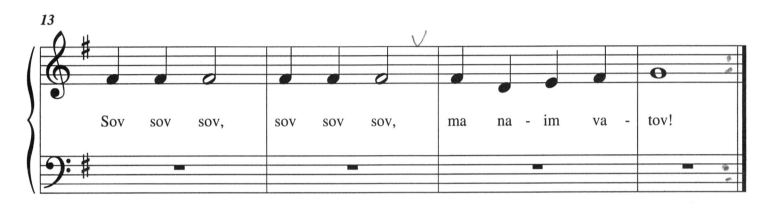

Sov sov sov,   sov sov sov,   ma na - im va - tov!

MA'OZ TZUR

(Rock of Ages)

*This song tells about the many times Israel fought for freedom
and the many times the people were made strong by their belief in God.*

TRADITIONAL
Arranged by DAVID KARP

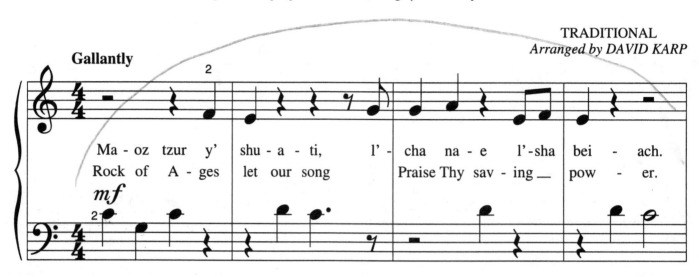

Ma - oz tzur y' shu - a - ti, l' - cha na - e l'-sha bei - ach.
Rock of A - ges let our song Praise Thy sav - ing — pow - er.

Accompaniment *(student plays one octave higher)*

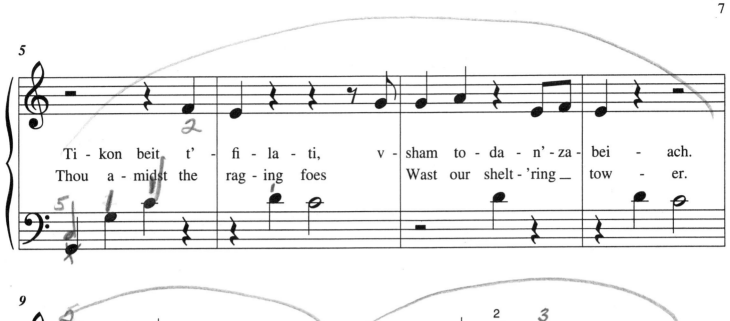

Ti - kon beit t' - fi - la - ti, v - sham to - da - n' - za - bei - ach.
Thou a - midst the rag - ing foes Wast our shelt - 'ring __ tow - er.

L'eit ta - chin mat - bei - ach, m' - tzur - ham' - na - bei - ach,
Fu - rious they as - sailed us, But thine arm a - vailed __ us,

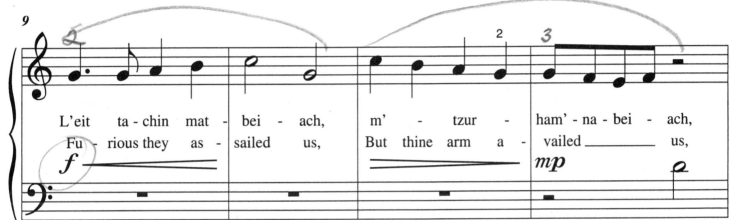

Awz eg - mor b' - shir miz - mor, Cha - nu - kat ha - miz - bei - ach.
And the word __ broke their sword __ When our own strength failed __ us.

Awz eg - mor b' - shir - miz - mor, Cha - nu - kat ha - miz - bei - ach.
And the word broke their sword __ When our own strength failed __ us.

O CHANUKAH, O CHANUKAH

This song celebrates lighting the menorah, eating latkes, and spinning dreidels.

TRADITIONAL
Arranged by DAVID KARP

BLESSING THE CHANUKAH CANDLES

These blessings are sung over the candles during Chanukah.

TRADITIONAL
Arranged by DAVID KARP

Ba - ruch a tah a - do - nai e - lo - hei - nu me-lech ha - o - lam { a -
{ she -

Accompaniment *(student plays one octave higher)*

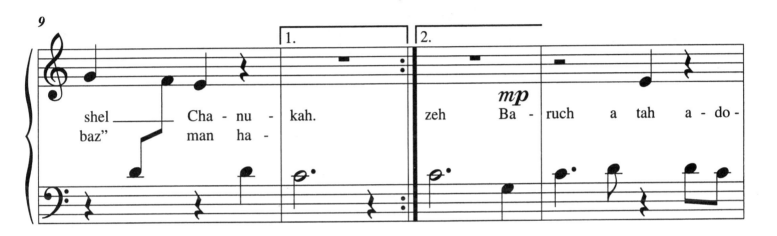

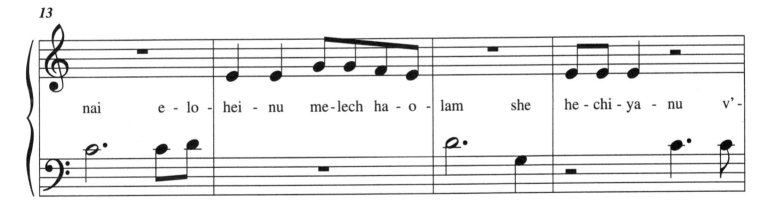

MY DREIDEL

A dreidel is a small top. There are special letters written on the four sides of the dreidel.
The letters mean "A Great Miracle Happened There."

S.E. GOLDFARB
Arranged by DAVID KARP

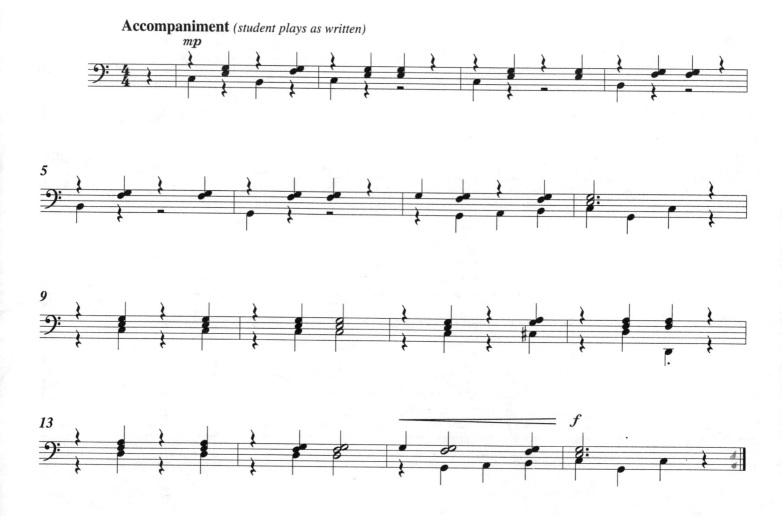

Verse 2:
It has a lovely body,
With leg so short and thin
And when it is all tired,
It drops and then I win.
(Chorus:)

Verse 3:
My dreidel's always playful,
It loves to dance and spin.
A happy game of dreidel,
Come play, now let's begin.
(Chorus:)

S'VIVON

This song tells about the miracle of Chanukah and how the candles burned for eight days and nights.

Words by L. KIPNIS

TRADITIONAL
Arranged by DAVID KARP

S' - vi - von sov sov sov Cha - nu - kah ___ hu chag tov

Accompaniment *(student plays one octave higher)*

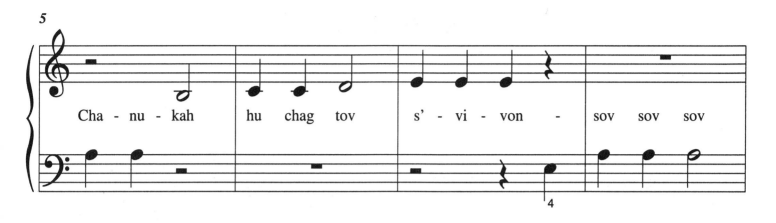

Cha - nu - kah   hu chag tov   s' - vi - von - sov sov sov

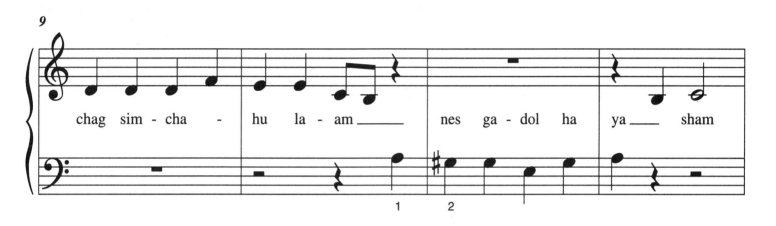

chag sim - cha - hu la - am ____ nes ga - dol ha ya ____ sham

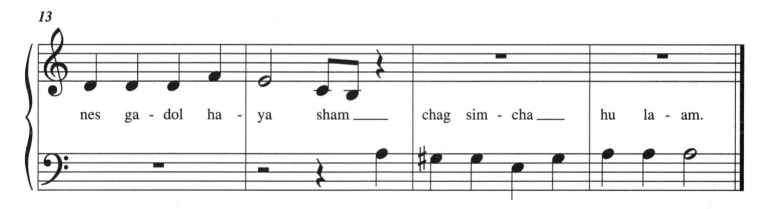

nes ga - dol ha - ya sham ____ chag sim - cha ____ hu la - am.

DAYEINU

This song is sung during the Passover Seder. It tells about the many gifts God gave the Jewish people
as they made their way out of slavery into freedom.

TRADITIONAL
Arranged by DAVID KARP

I - lu   ho - tzi   ho - tzi - a - nu   ho - tzi - a - nu   mi mitz - ra - yim

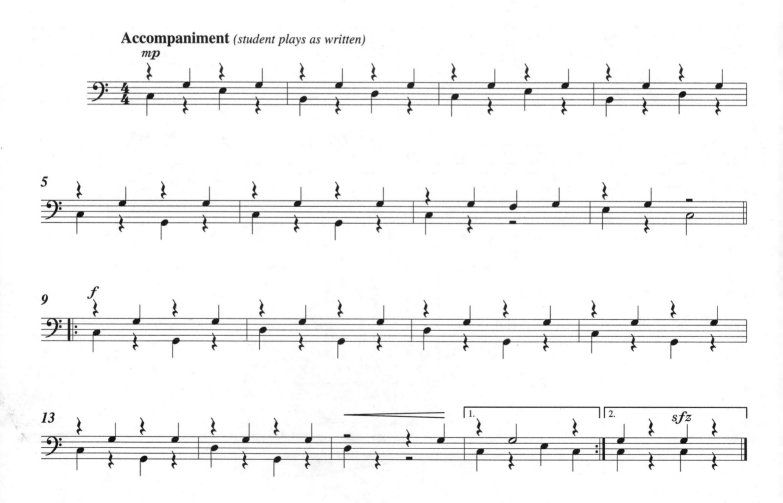

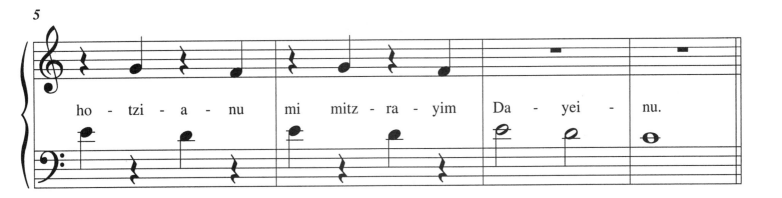

5

ho - tzi - a - nu   mi   mitz - ra - yim   Da - yei - nu.

9

f

Da   da - yei - nu,   Da   da - yei - nu,

13

Da   da - yei - nu,   Da - yei - nu   da - yei - nu   da - yei - nu   nu!   *sfz*

1.   2.

EILIYAHU HANAVI

Elijah is a prophet. He is a welcome guest at the Seder. He brings hope and peace.

TRADITIONAL
Arranged by DAVID KARP

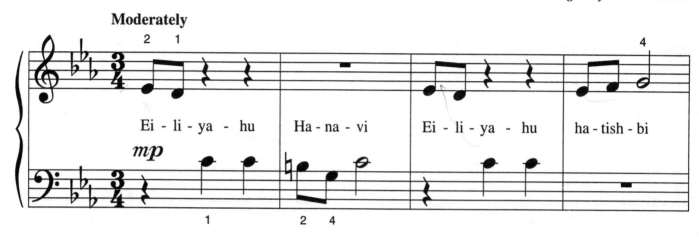

Ei - li - ya - hu   Ha - na - vi   Ei - li - ya - hu   ha - tish - bi

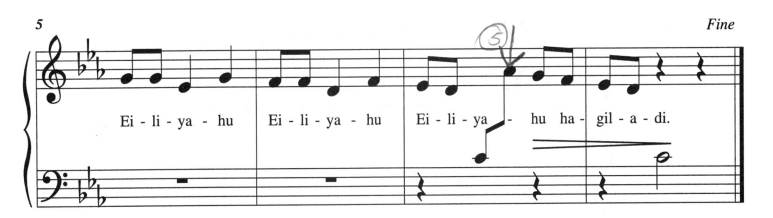

Fine

Ei - li - ya - hu   Ei - li - ya - hu   Ei - li - ya - hu ha - gil - a - di.

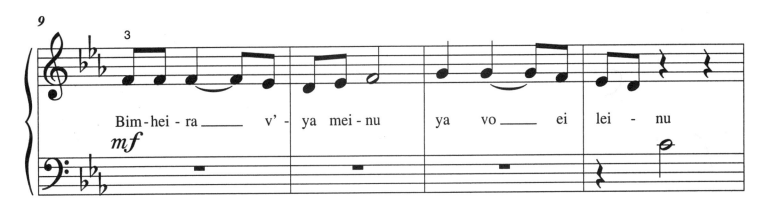

3

Bim - hei - ra _____ v' - ya mei - nu   ya vo _____ ei lei - nu

mf

D.C. al Fine

Im Ma - shi - ach ben Da - vid   Im Ma - shi - ach ben Da - vid.

MA NISHTANA?

During the Seder the youngest child asks the Four Questions.
The questions asked: Why is this night different from all other nights? The rest of the Seder answers the questions.

TRADITIONAL
Arranged by DAVID KARP

Moderately, with expression

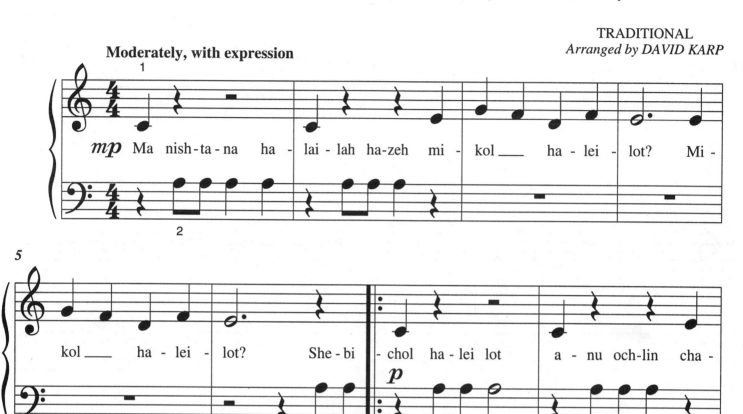

Accompaniment *(student plays one octave higher)*

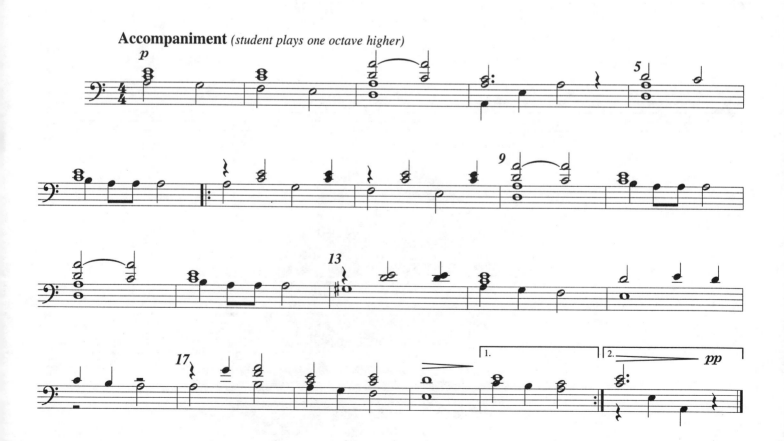

Verse 2:
She-b'chol ha-lei-lot, a-nu och-lin,
Sh-ar-y-ra-kot, sh-ar-y-ra-kot,
Ha-lai-lah, ha-zeh, ha-lai-lah, ha-zeh, ku-lo, ma-ror,
Ha-lai-lah, ha-zeh, ha-lai-lah, ha-zeh, ku-lo, ma-ror.

Verse 3:
She-b'chol ha-lei-lot, ein-a-nu, mat-bei-lin
A-fi-lu-pa-am e-chat, a-fi-lu-pa-am e-chat,
Ha-lai-lah, ha-zeh, ha-lai-lah, ha-zeh, sh-tei f'-a-mim,
Ha-lai-lah, ha-zeh, ha-lai-lah, ha-zeh, sh-tei f'-a-mim.

Verse 4:
She-b'chol ha-lei-lot, a-nu och-lin
Bein yosh-vin u-vein m'-su-bin, bein yosh-vin u-vein m'-su-bin.
Ha-lai-lah, ha-zeh, ha-lai-lah, ha-zeh, ku-la-nu m'-su-bin.
Ha-lai-lah, ha-zeh, ha-lai-lah, ha-zeh, ku-la-nu m'-su-bin.

Translation: Why is this night different from all other nights?

On all other nights we eat either leavened bread or matzah; on this night we eat only matzah.
On all other nights we eat all kinds of herbs; on this night we eat bitter herbs.
On all other nights we do not dip herbs at all; on this night we dip them twice.
On all other nights we eat in an ordinary manner; on this night we eat with special ceremony.

CHAD GADYA

This is one of the songs that is sung at the end of the Passover Seder.
The "kid" (goat) is bought by the father and represents the people of Israel.
It is a challenge (and fun!) to remember all the verses.

TRADITIONAL
Arranged by DAVID KARP

In a flowing manner

1. Chad gad - ya _____ chad gad - ya My
2. Chad gad - ya _____ chad gad - ya There

fa - ther bought for two _____ zu - zim my
came a cat and ate ____ the ____ kid my

Accompaniment (*student plays as written*)

sempre staccato

CHAD GADYA

The following verses are usually half spoken and half sung.
As the song progresses, it usually turns into a race between the young and the old to see who can finish first.

1. Chad Gadya, Chad Gadya,
   My father bought for two zuzim,
   Chad Gadya, Chad Gadya

2. There came a cat and ate the kid,
   My father bought for two zuzim,
   Chad Gadya, Chad Gadya

3. Then came a dog and bit the cat
   That ate the kid,
   My father bought for two zuzim,
   Chad Gadya, Chad Gadya

4. Then came the stick and beat the dog
   That bit the cat
   That ate the kid,
   My father bought for two zuzim,
   Chad Gadya, Chad Gadya

5. Then came the fire and burned the stick,
   That beat the dog
   That bit the cat
   That ate the kid,
   My father bought for two zuzim,
   Chad Gadya, Chad Gadya

6. Then came the water and quenched the fire,
   That burned the stick,
   That beat the dog
   That bit the cat
   That ate the kid,
   My father bought for two zuzim,
   Chad Gadya, Chad Gadya

7. Then came the ox and drank the water,
   That quenched the fire,
   That burned the stick,
   That beat the dog
   That bit the cat
   That ate the kid,
   My father bought for two zuzim,
   Chad Gadya, Chad Gadya

8. Then came the butcher and killed the ox
   That drank the water,
   That quenched the fire,
   That burned the stick,
   That beat the dog
   That bit the cat
   That ate the kid,
   My father bought for two zuzim,
   Chad Gadya, Chad Gadya

9. Then came the angel of death and slew the butcher
   Who killed the ox
   That drank the water,
   That quenched the fire,
   That burned the stick,
   That beat the dog
   That bit the cat
   That ate the kid,
   My father bought for two zuzim,
   Chad Gadya, Chad Gadya

10. Then came the Holy One, blest be He
    And destroyed the angel of death,
    That slew the butcher
    Who killed the ox
    That drank the water,
    That quenched the fire,
    That burned the stick,
    That beat the dog
    That bit the cat
    That ate the kid,
    My father bought for two zuzim,
    Chad Gadya, Chad Gadya

CHAG PURIM

Purim is a day for fun. People celebrate by wearing costumes,
using noisemakers (gragger) and eating hamantashen.

TRADITIONAL
Arranged by DAVID KARP

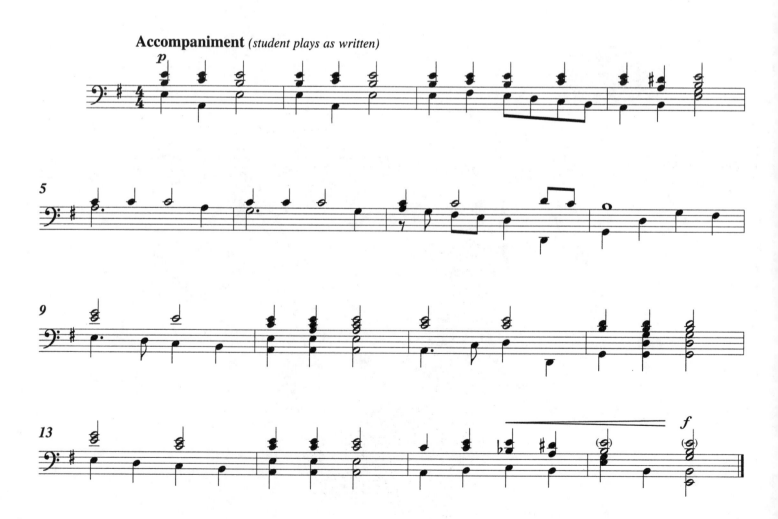

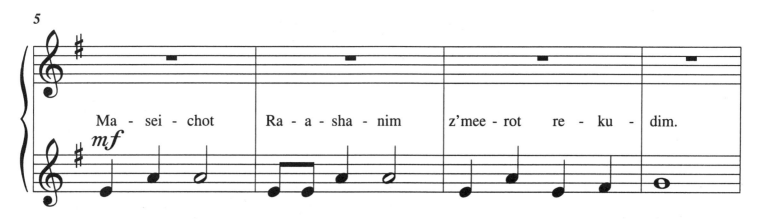

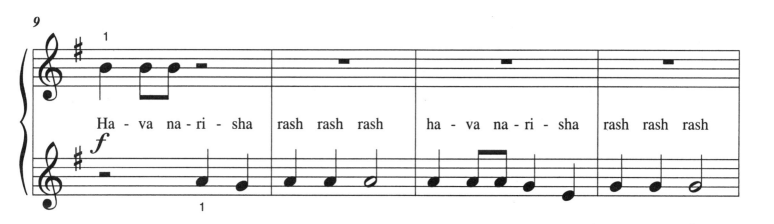

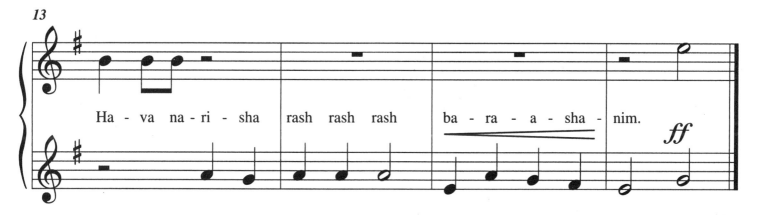

5

Ma - sei - chot | Ra - a - sha - nim | z'mee - rot re - ku - dim.

9

Ha - va na - ri - sha | rash rash rash | ha - va na - ri - sha | rash rash rash

13

Ha - va na - ri - sha | rash rash rash | ba - ra - a - sha - nim.

HAMAN, A WICKED MAN

The people are happy that there is no longer an evil Haman.

TRADITIONAL
Arranged by DAVID KARP

With a bounce!

Oh once there was a wick-ed wick-ed man and Ha-man was his name, sir. He

Accompaniment *(student plays as written)*

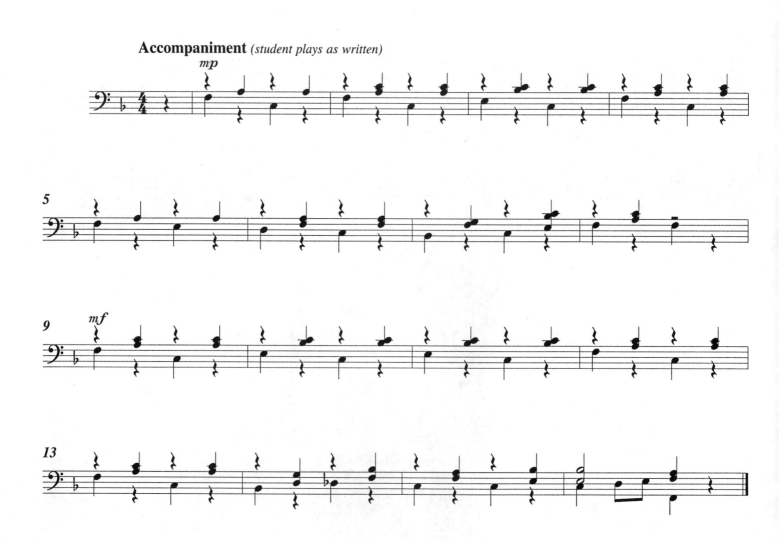

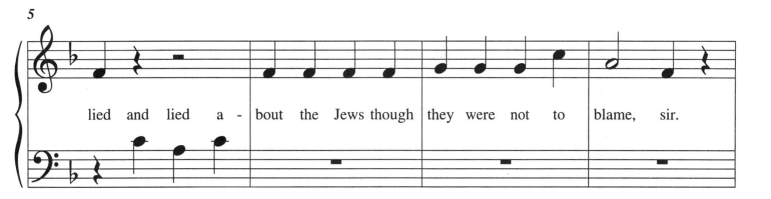

lied and lied a - bout the Jews though they were not to blame, sir.

Oh, to-day we'll mer-ry mer-ry be, Oh, to-day we'll mer-ry mer-ry be,

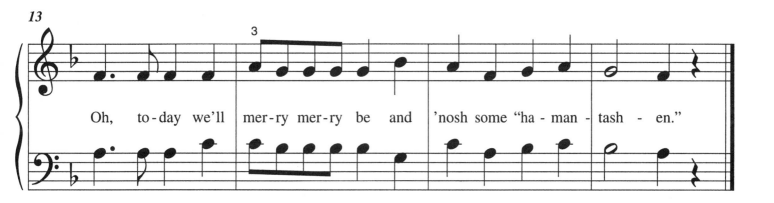

Oh, to-day we'll mer-ry mer-ry be and 'nosh some "ha - man - tash - en."

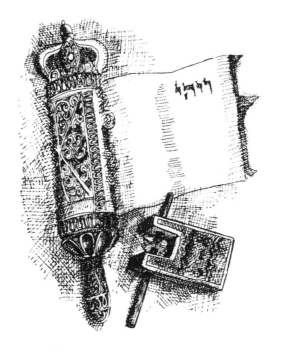

ARTZA ALINU

This song tells about how the early Israeli pioneers grew vegetables.

TRADITIONAL
Arranged by DAVID KARP

Accompaniment *(student plays one octave higher)*

HATIKVA (THE HOPE)

A man by the name of Natali Herz Imber (1856-1911) wrote this poem.
It is now the national anthem of the State of Israel.

TRADITIONAL
Arranged by DAVID KARP

Kol - od ba-lei vav p'ni - ma. Ne-fesh ye-hu - di ho - mi - yah. U'-

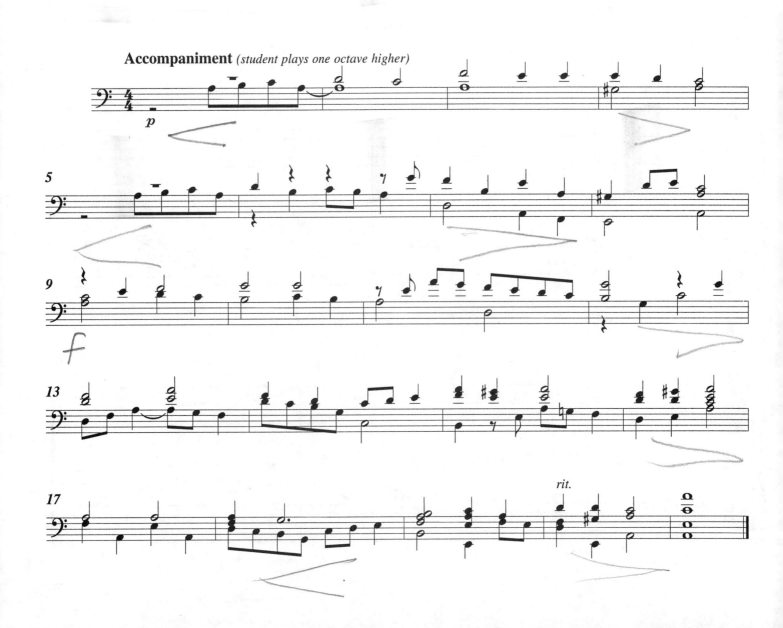

Accompaniment *(student plays one octave higher)*

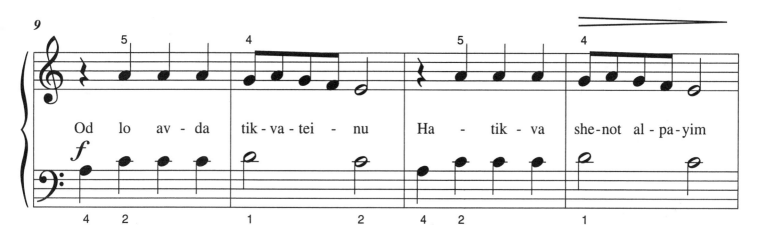

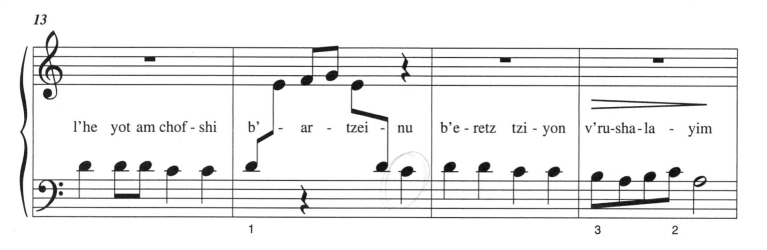

HAVA NAGILA

This is one of the most popular folk songs of Israel. It invites us to be joyful as we dance and sing.

TRADITIONAL
Arranged by DAVID KARP

HEIVEINU SHALOM ALEICHEM

Shalom in Hebrew means hello, goodbye and peace. This short song of welcome says "Peace unto you."

TRADITIONAL
Arranged by DAVID KARP

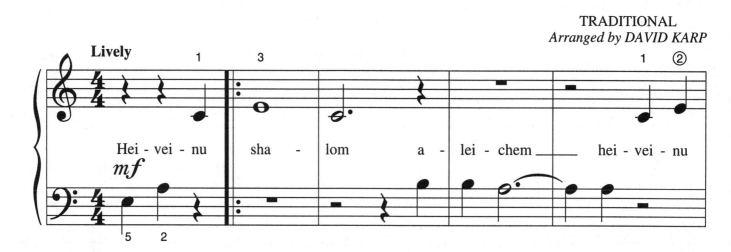

Hei - vei - nu   sha - lom   a - lei - chem ____ hei - vei - nu

Accompaniment *(student plays one octave higher)*

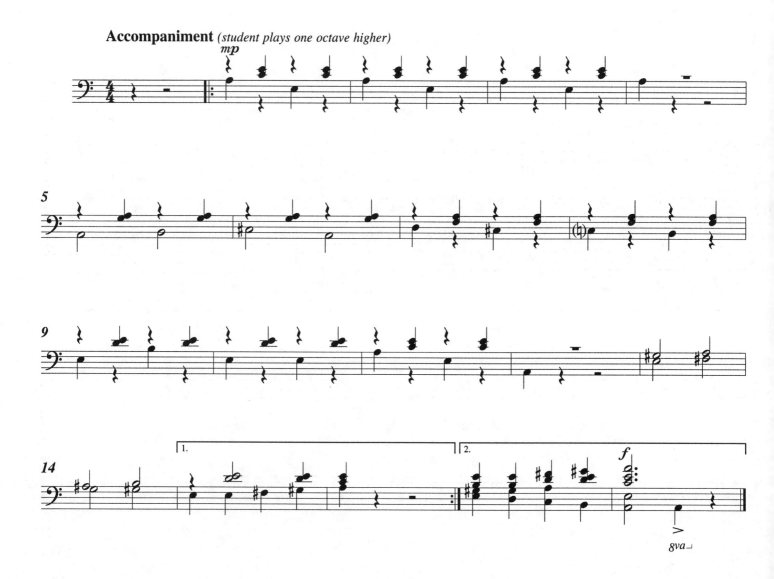

8va⌐

shalom aleichem heiveinu

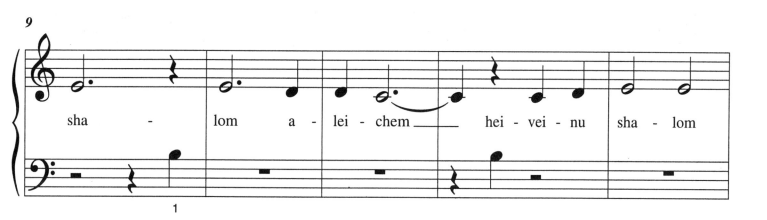

shalom aleichem heiveinu shalom

shalom shalom aleichem heiveinu shalom aleichem!

OSE SHALOM

a prayer for peace

TRADITIONAL
Arranged by DAVID KARP

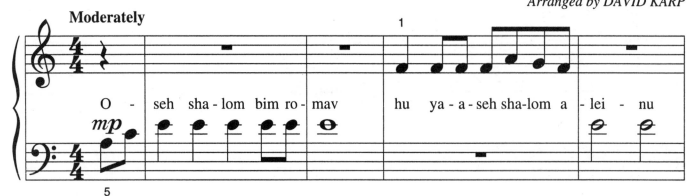

O - seh sha - lom bim ro - mav hu ya - a - seh sha-lom a - lei - nu

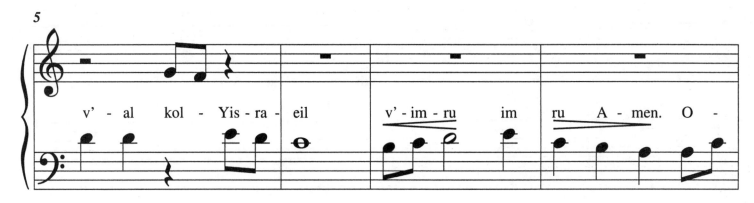

v' - al kol - Yis - ra - eil v' - im - ru im ru A - men. O -

Accompaniment *(student plays one octave higher)*

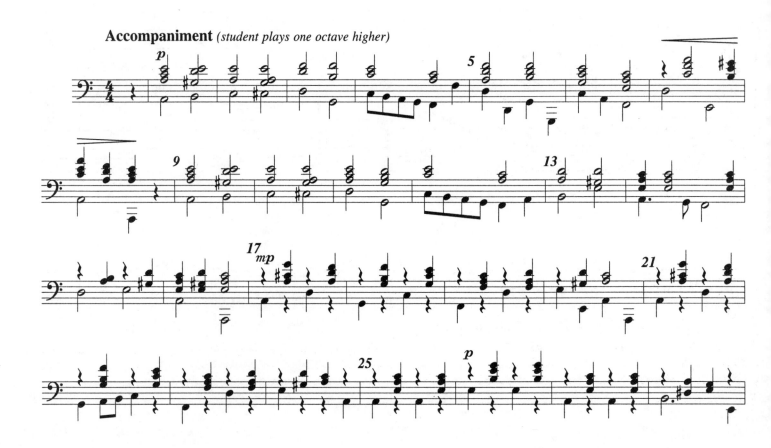

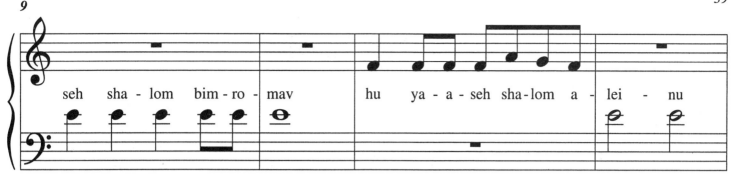

seh sha - lom bim - ro - mav   hu ya - a - seh sha - lom a - lei - nu

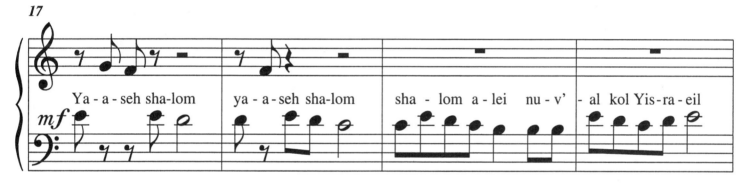

v' al kol - Yis - ra - eil   v' im - ru im - ru A - men.

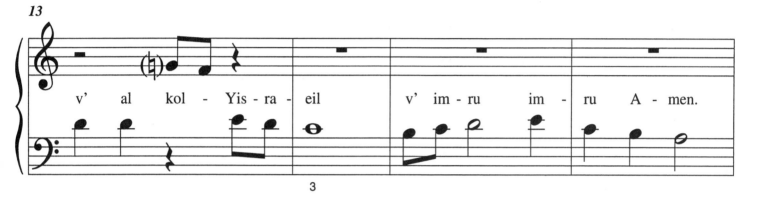

Ya - a - seh sha - lom   ya - a - seh sha - lom   sha - lom a - lei nu - v' - al kol Yis - ra - eil

mf

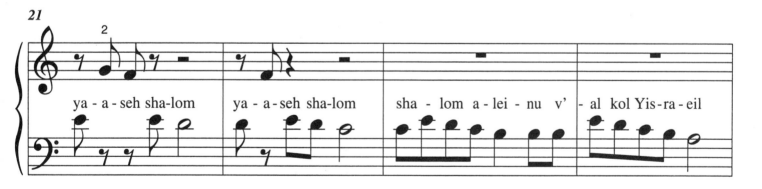

ya - a - seh sha - lom   ya - a - seh sha - lom   sha - lom a - lei - nu v' - al kol Yis - ra - eil

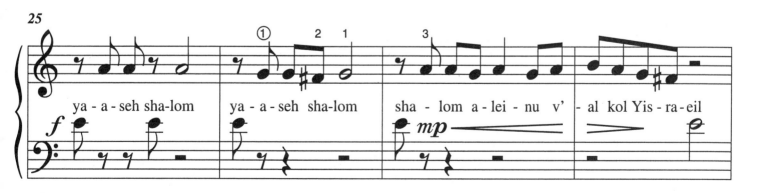

ya - a - seh sha - lom   ya - a - seh sha - lom   sha - lom a - lei - nu v' - al kol Yis - ra - eil

f   *mp*

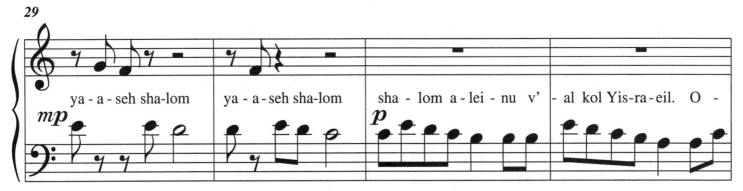

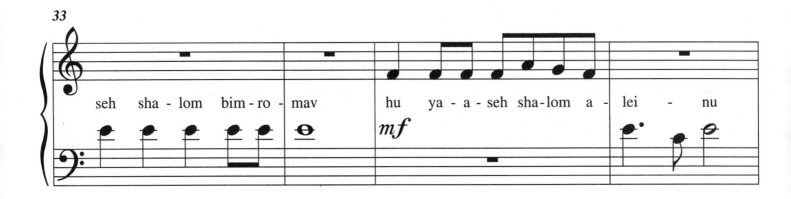

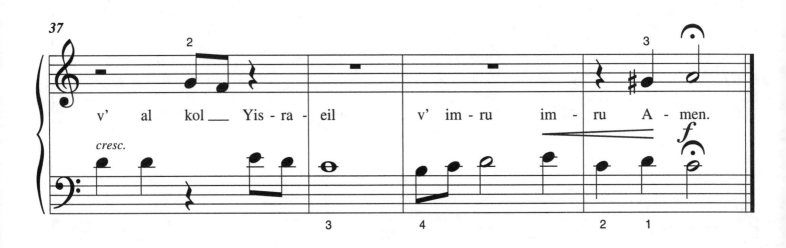

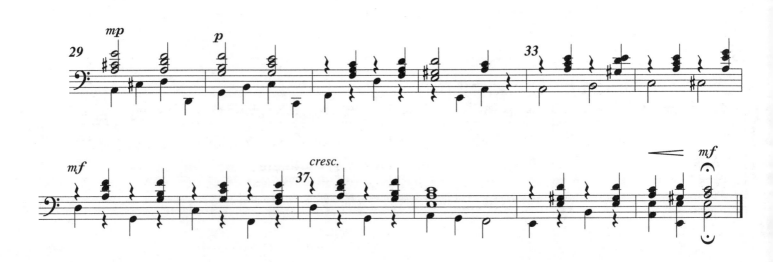

SH'MA YISRAEIL

The Sh'ma is often called the "watchword of the Jewish faith."
It is recited at worship services and is one of the most important prayers.

TRADITIONAL
Arranged by DAVID KARP

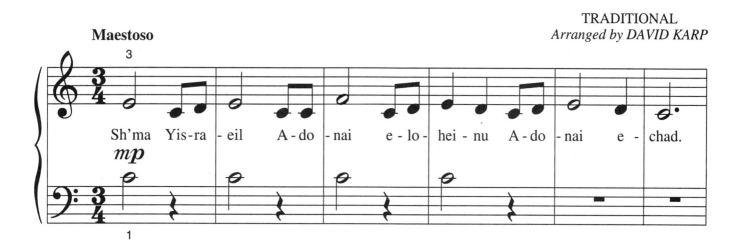

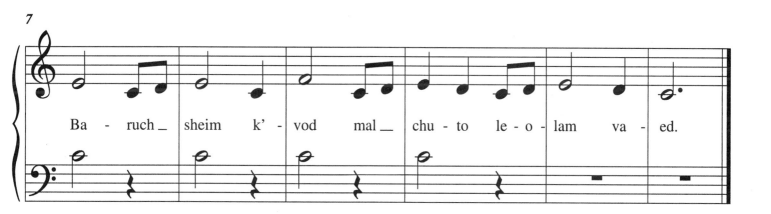

EIN KEILOHEINU

This song is very popular and is sung at the end of the Sabbath Service.
It was composed a long, long time ago.

TRADITIONAL
Arranged by DAVID KARP

Ein kei - lo - hei - nu, ein ka - do nei - nu,

ein ke - mal kei - nu, ein ke - mo - shi - ei - nu.

Accompaniment *(student plays as written)*

ADON OLAM

There are many melodies for this song. It has been in the prayerbook for 600 years.
This is the most popular melody for this song.

TRADITIONAL
Arranged by DAVID KARP

A - don O - lam   a - sher ma - lach   B' - te - rem kol   ye - tsir niv - ra   Le -

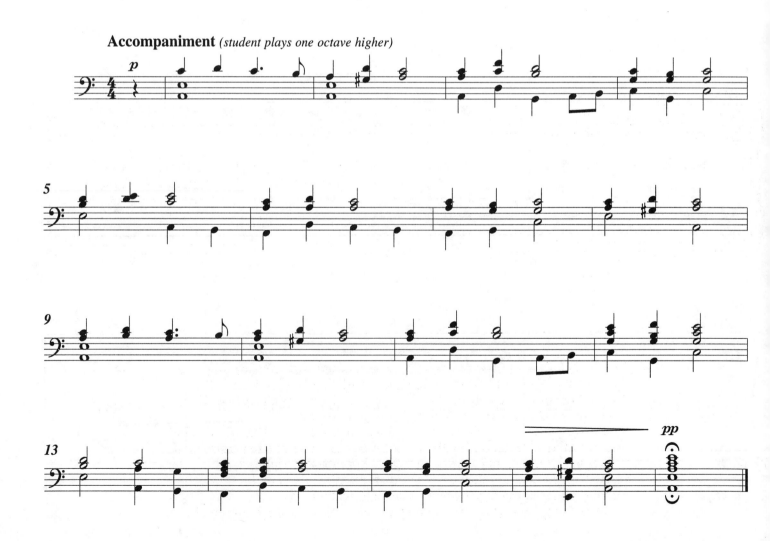

Accompaniment *(student plays one octave higher)*

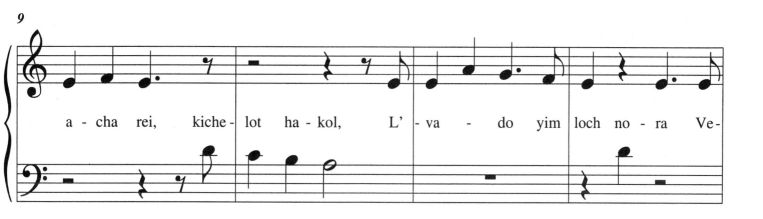

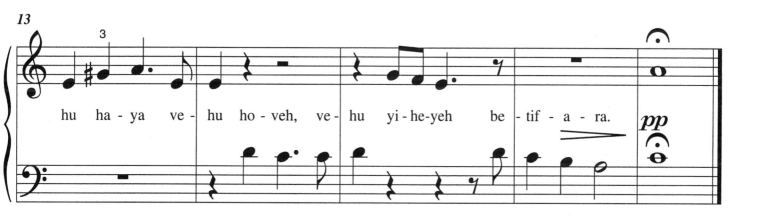

Adon Olam

God is the eternal Lord who ruled before anything was created.

At that time when all was made by God's will, God was called ruler.

And at that end, when all shall cease to be, God alone shall still be King.

God was, God is, and God shall be in glorious eternity.

God is one and there is no other to compare to God or to place beside God.

God is without beginning, without end. All power and rule belong to God.

God is my living redeemer, my stronghold in times of trouble.

God is my guide and refuge, my share of joy in the day I call.

To God I entrust my spirit when I sleep and when I wake.

As long as my soul is within my body, God is with me and I am not afraid.

HINEI MA TOV

Behold how good and pleasant it is for brothers (friends) to be together.

TRADITIONAL
Arranged by DAVID KARP

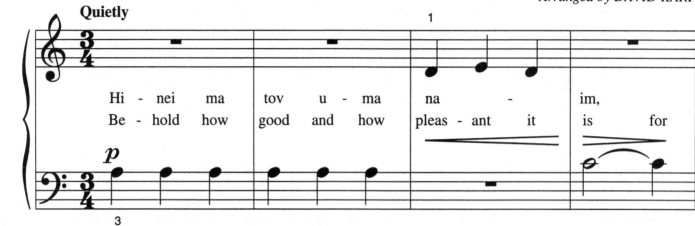

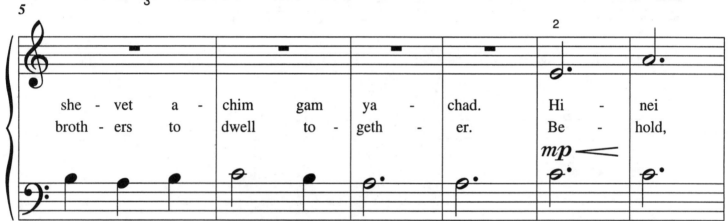

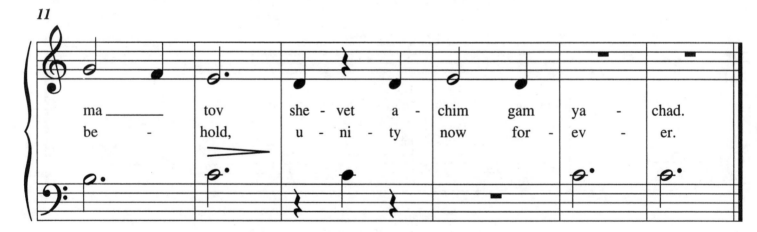

Accompaniment *(student plays one octave higher)*

Chanukah

Chanukah is celebrated for eight days and is called the Festival of Lights. This holiday is about religious freedom.

Each night, the candles on the menorah are lit and prayers are said. After the prayers, songs are sung, games are played and potato latkes (pancakes) and jelly donuts are eaten.

Passover

Passover is a story about freedom, God, a man called Moses, and the Jewish people. Moses, with God's help, frees the people from being slaves in Egypt.

During Passover there is a special meal called the Seder. At this meal a story is told and special foods are eaten.

Purim

Purim is a time when people are very happy. They listen to a story read from a scroll. People go to carnivals and parties and wear costumes. They make loud noises with a noisemaker (greggar) when the name of Haman, a wicked man, is read from the scroll. People eat a special pastry called hamentashen. It looks like a triangle and is filled with fruit. During this festival people send gifts to friends and help the poor.

Folk Songs

The founding of the State of Isreal is a wonderful and exciting story. The early settlers worked hard at building during the day and at night they celebrated by singing songs and dancing.

Music from the Synagogue

Music is a very important part of prayer. Many songs are sung during the prayer service.

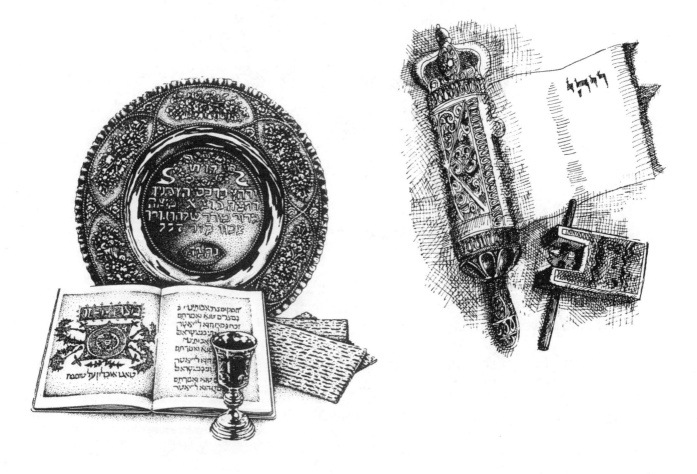